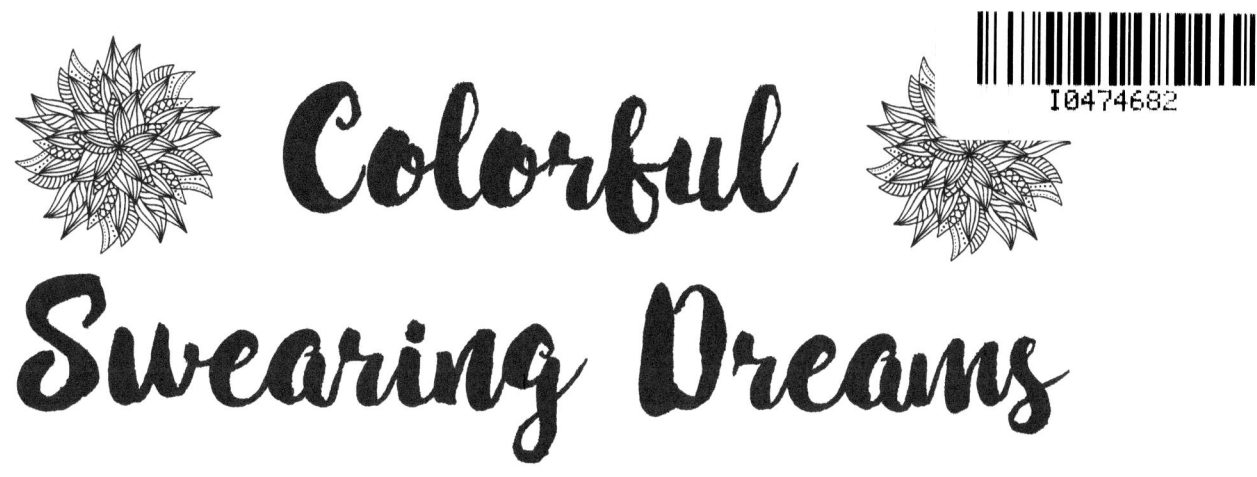

# Colorful
# Swearing Dreams
## Swear Word Coloring Book for Adults

## IS YOUR STRESS LEVEL HIGH?
## DO YOU WANT TO SWEAR OUT LOUD
## TO LEVEL IT DOWN?
## THIS BOOK WILL KICK YOUR STRESS AWAY!

Multiple studies revealed that coloring mandalas, geometric patterns & other shapes helps reduce stress and anxiety for adults.

This swear word coloring book will allow you to enter in a relaxed state by focusing in what you are doing and blocking out the nonstop thinking or other distractions. Those swear word designs will make you laugh and relieve your stress by expelling your negative thoughts.

This book contains 20 pages of beautiful & intricate designs mixing up with funny swear words that will connect with you.
Each page is single-sided for getting the best coloring experience.

## TIME TO COLOR THE STRESS AWAY!

# Colorful Swearing Dreams

## Swear Word Coloring Book for Adults

# Coloring Test Page

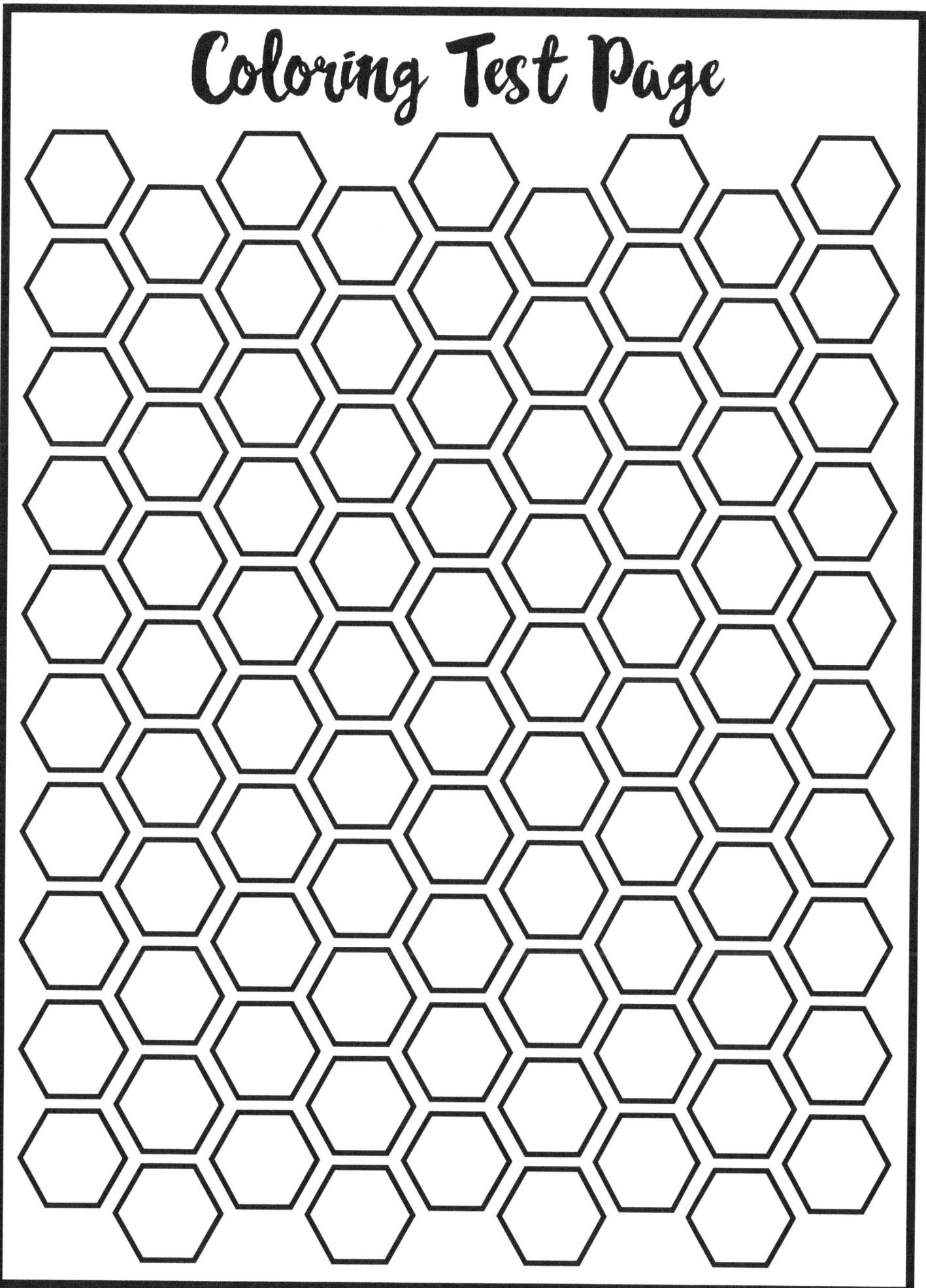

# Colorful Swearing Dreams

Swear Word Coloring Book for Adults

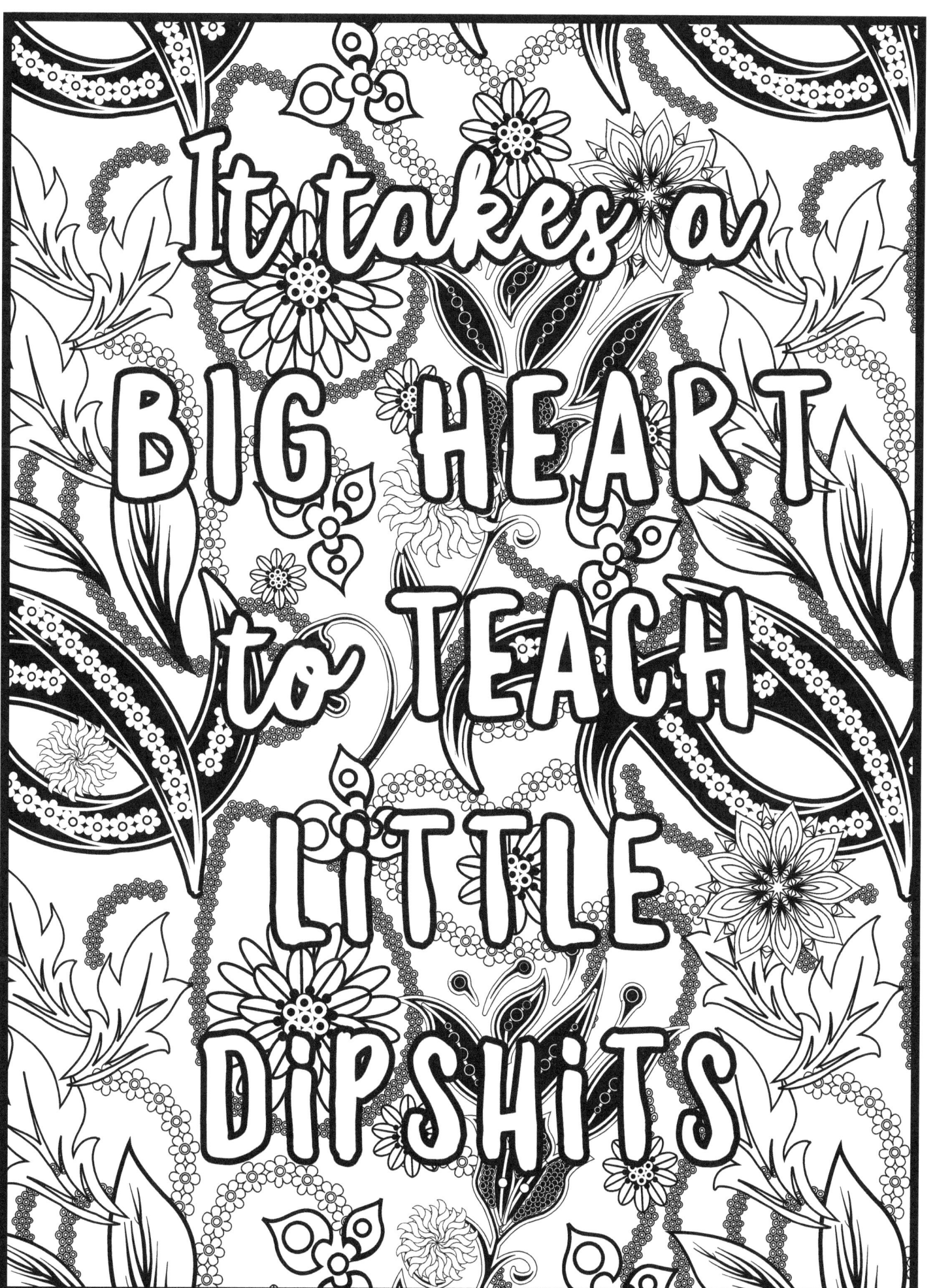

# Colorful Swearing Dreams

### Swear Word Coloring Book for Adults

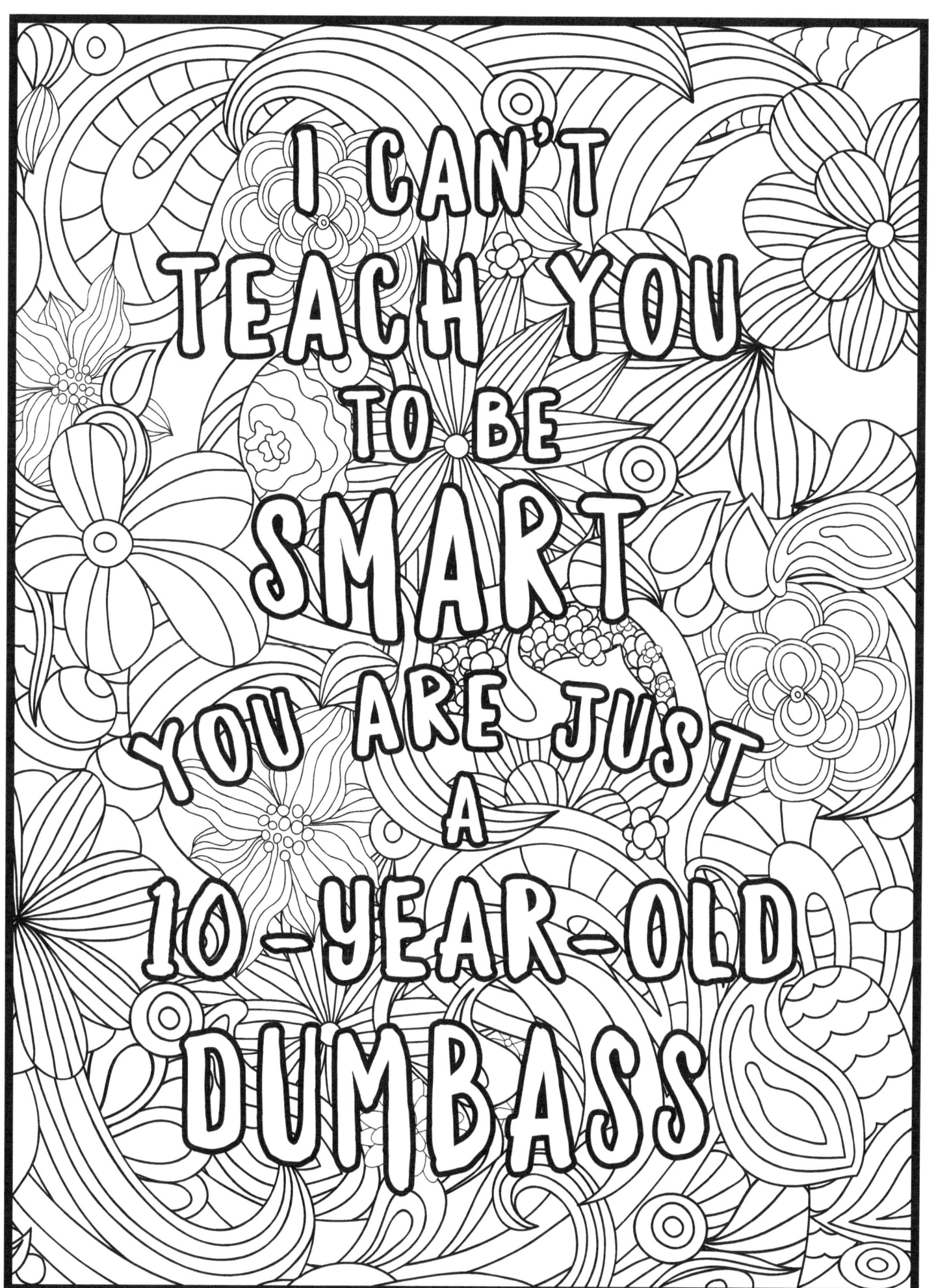

# Colorful Swearing Dreams

### Swear Word Coloring Book for Adults

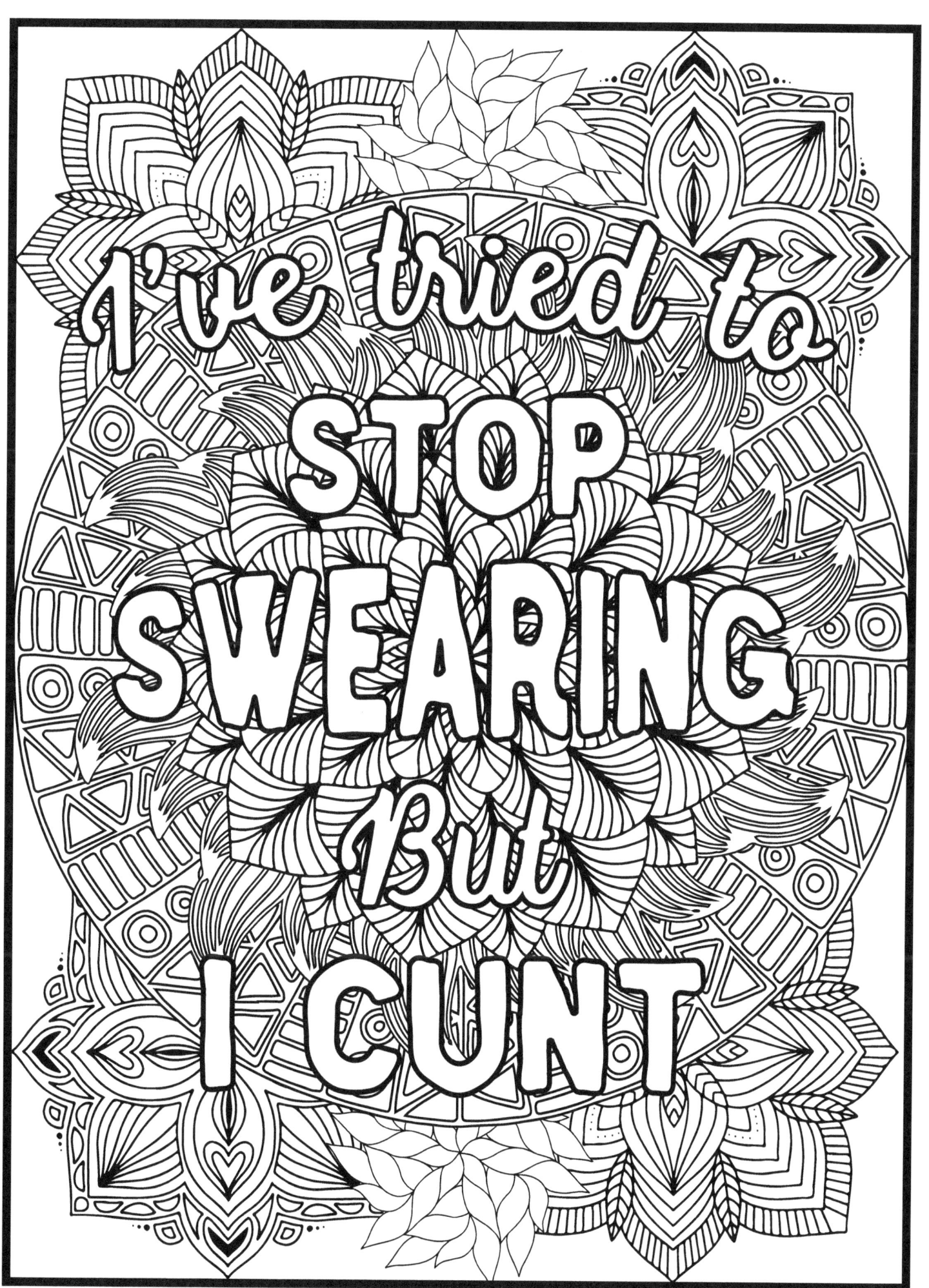

# Colorful Swearing Dreams

Swear Word Coloring Book for Adults

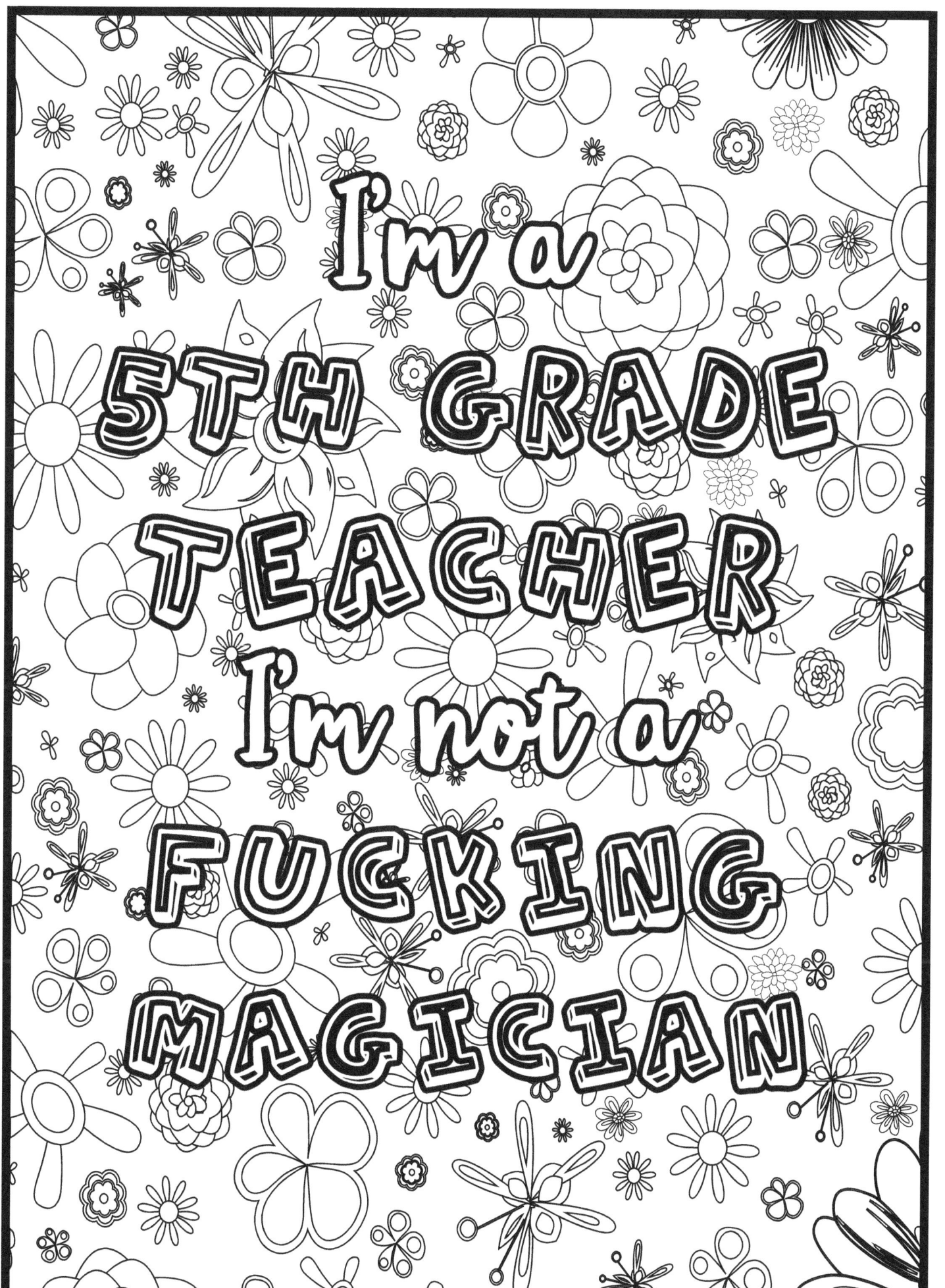

# Colorful

# Swearing Dreams

Swear Word Coloring Book for Adults

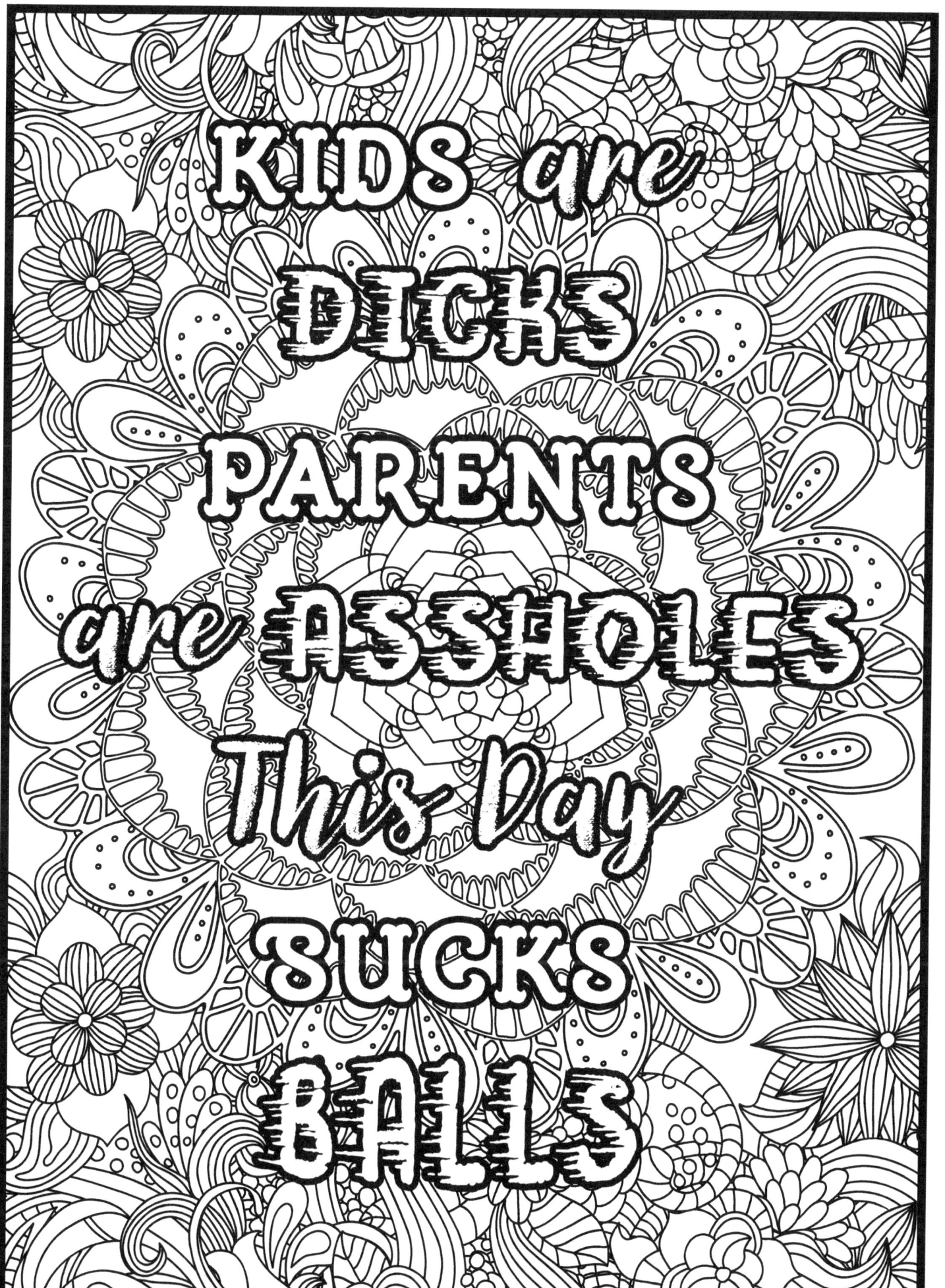

# Colorful Swearing Dreams

## Swear Word Coloring Book for Adults

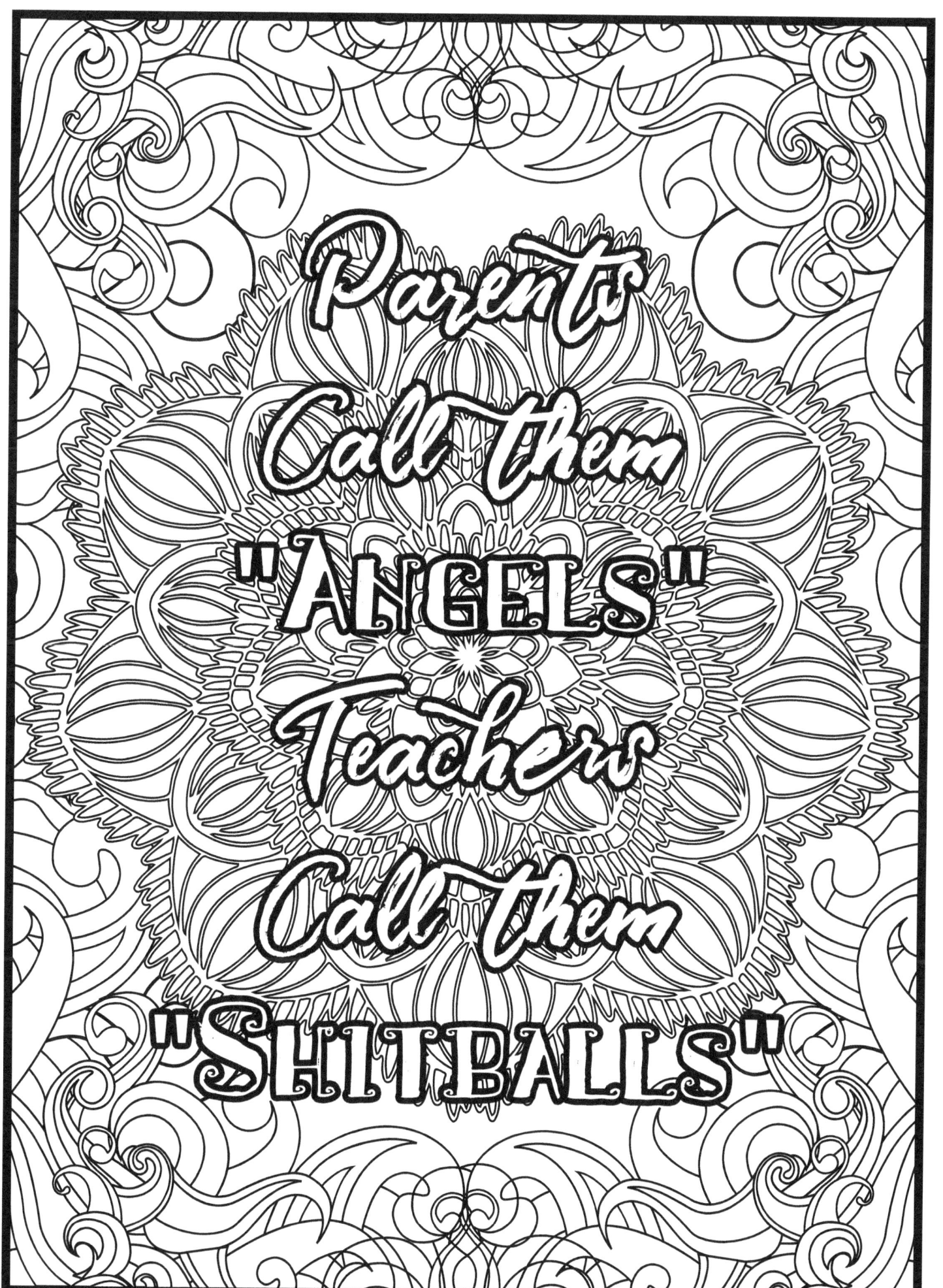

# Colorful Swearing Dreams

## Swear Word Coloring Book for Adults

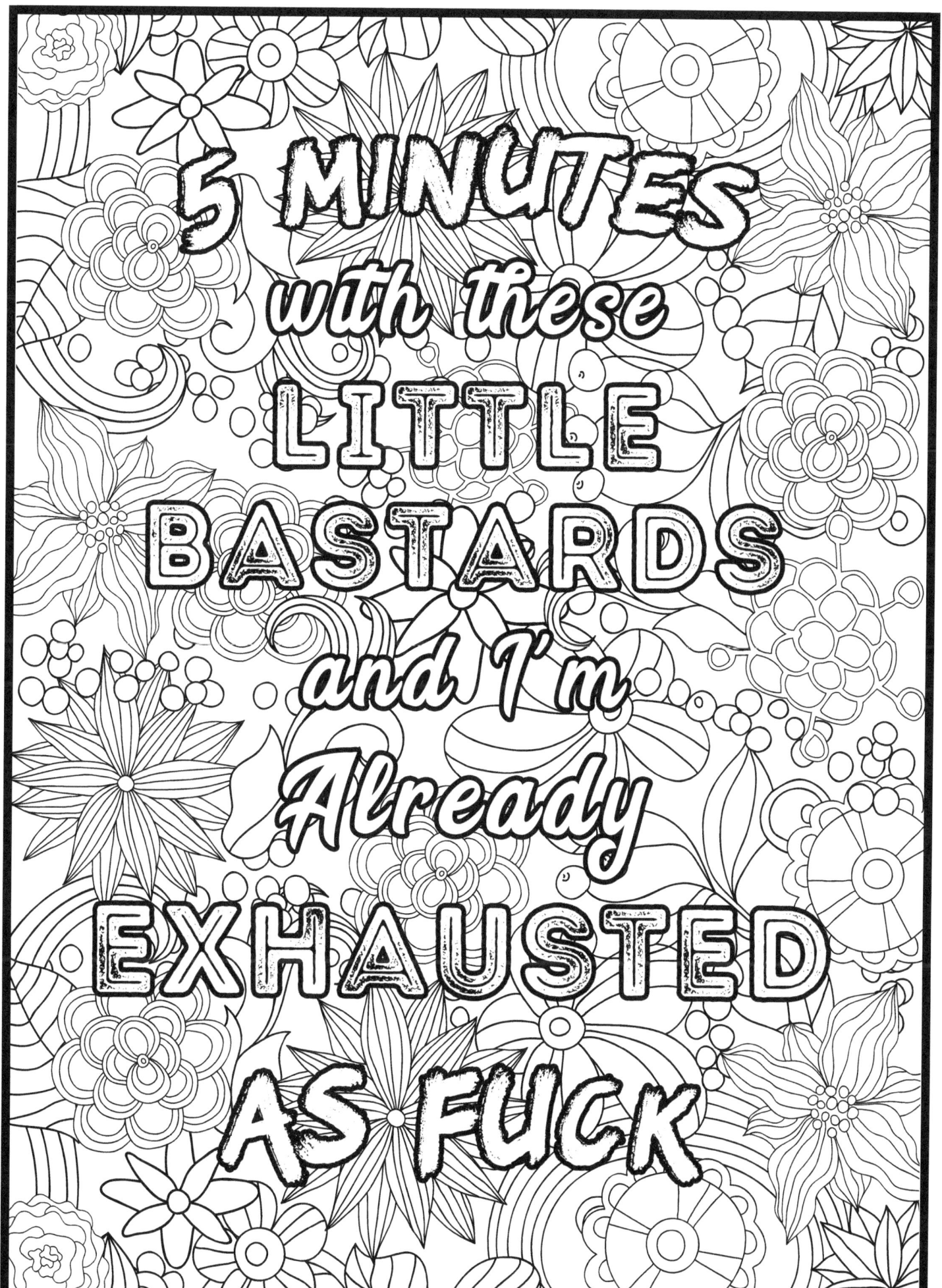

# Colorful Swearing Dreams

Swear Word Coloring Book for Adults

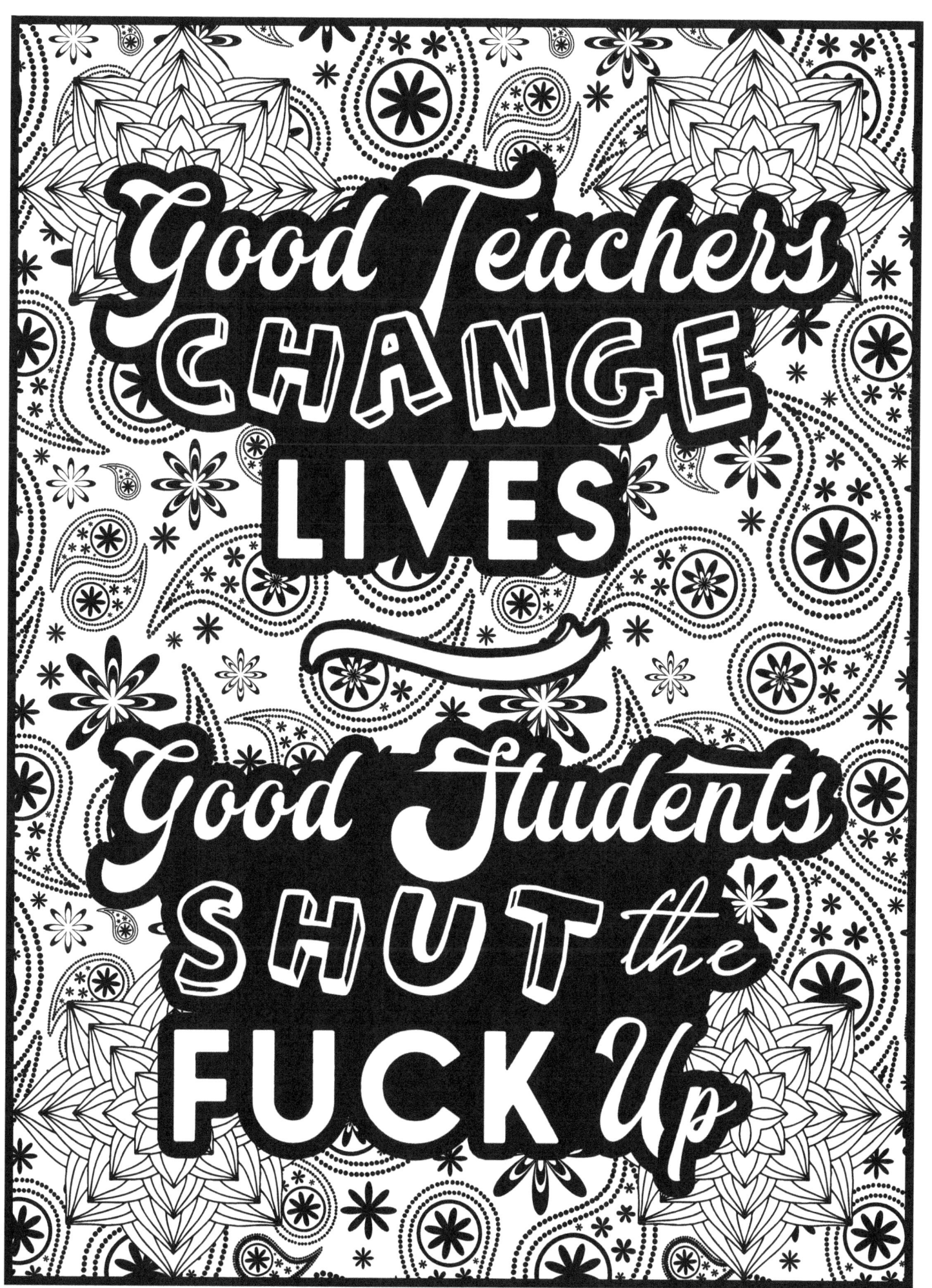

# Colorful

# Swearing Dreams

Swear Word Coloring Book for Adults

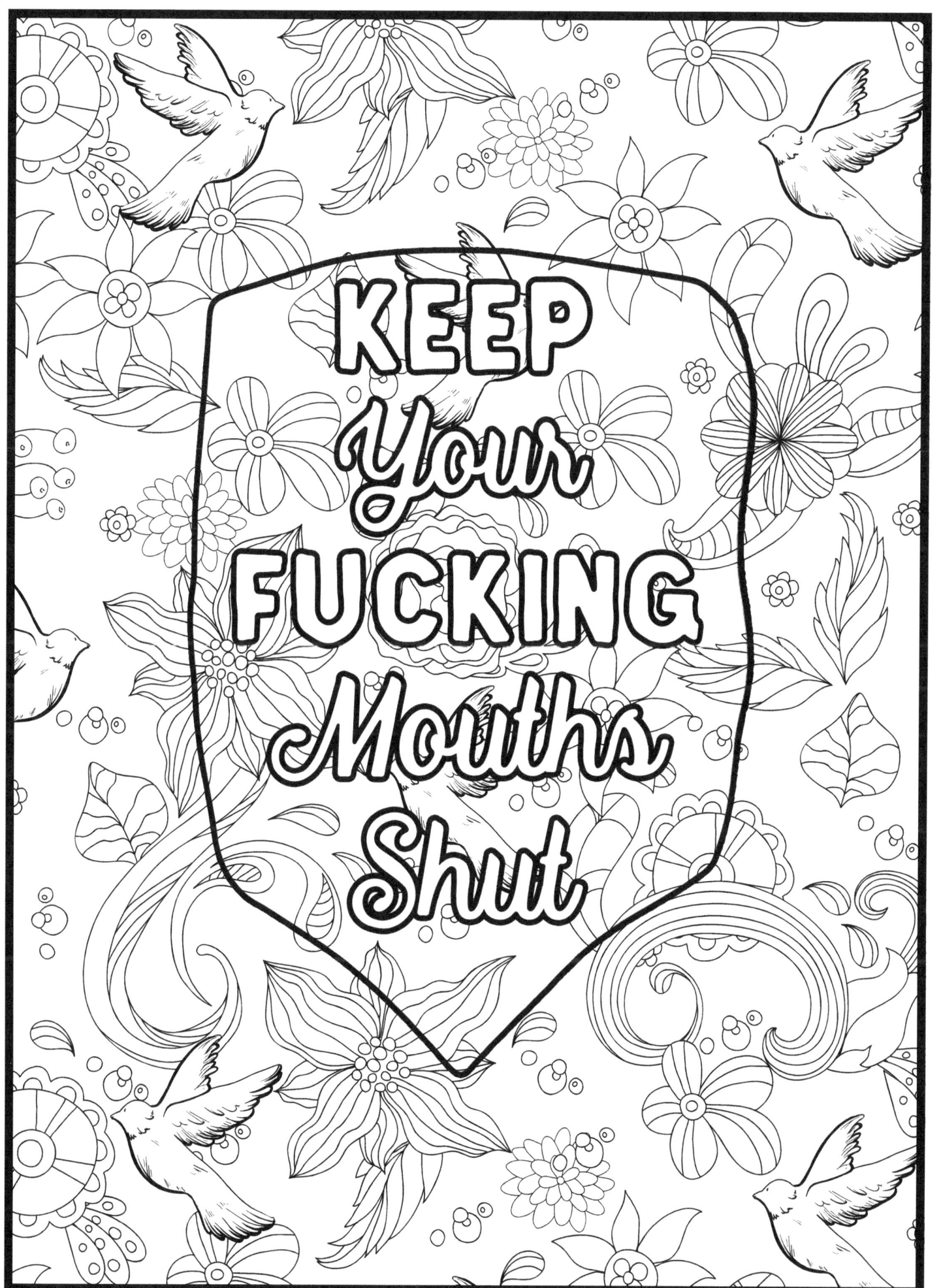

# Colorful Swearing Dreams

### Swear Word Coloring Book for Adults

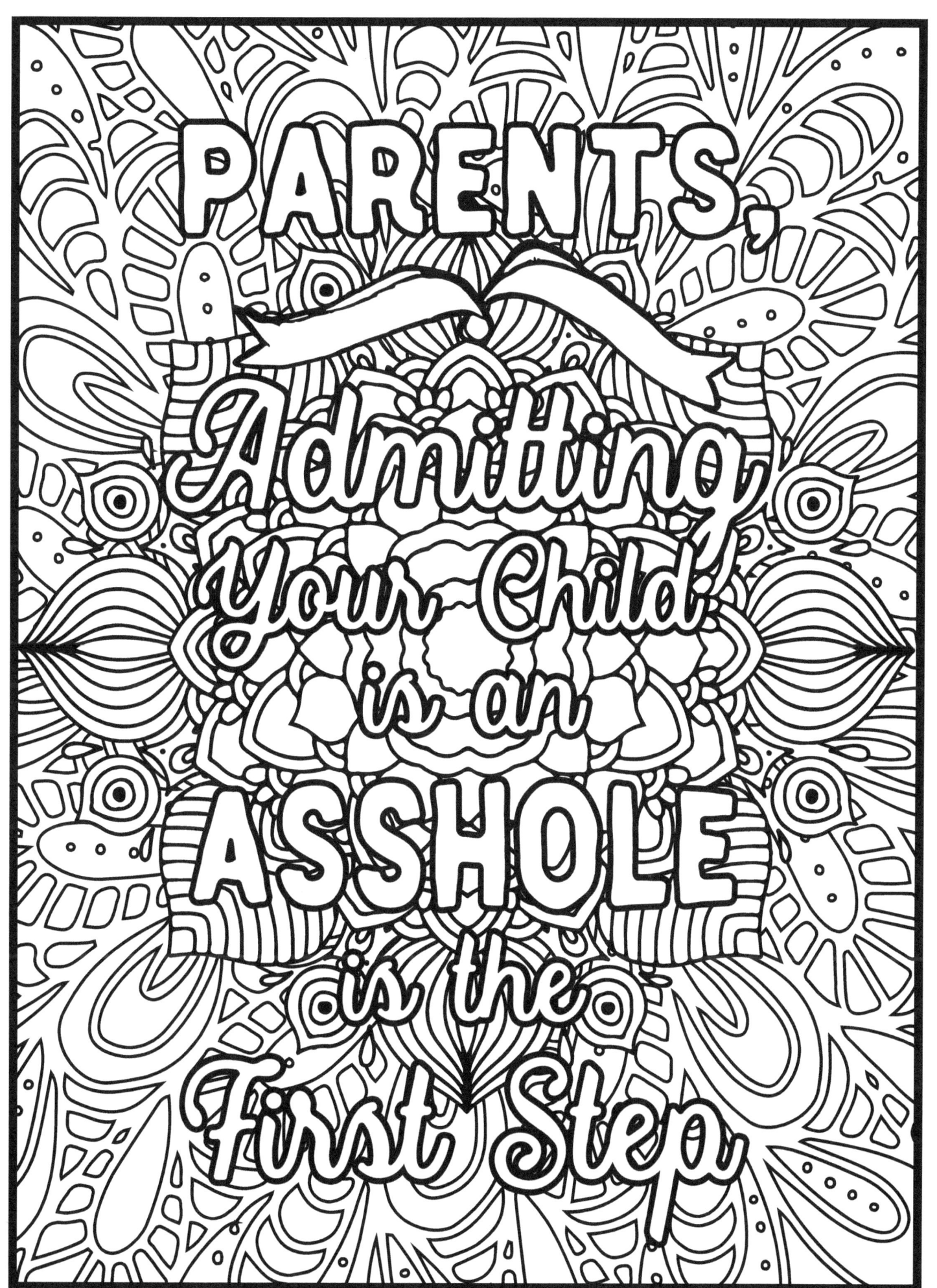

# Colorful

# Swearing Dreams

Swear Word Coloring Book for Adults

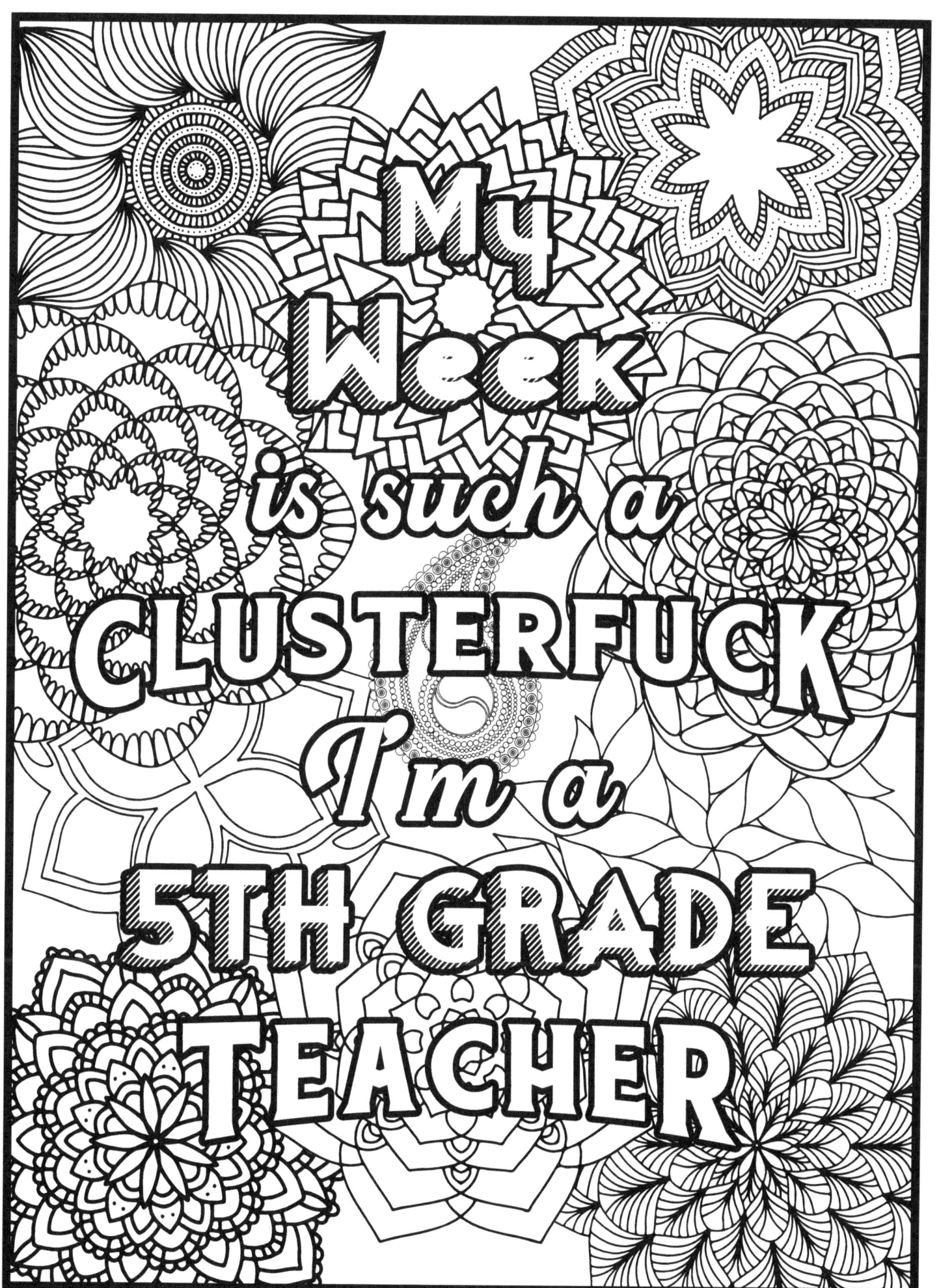

# Colorful

# Swearing Dreams

## Swear Word Coloring Book for Adults

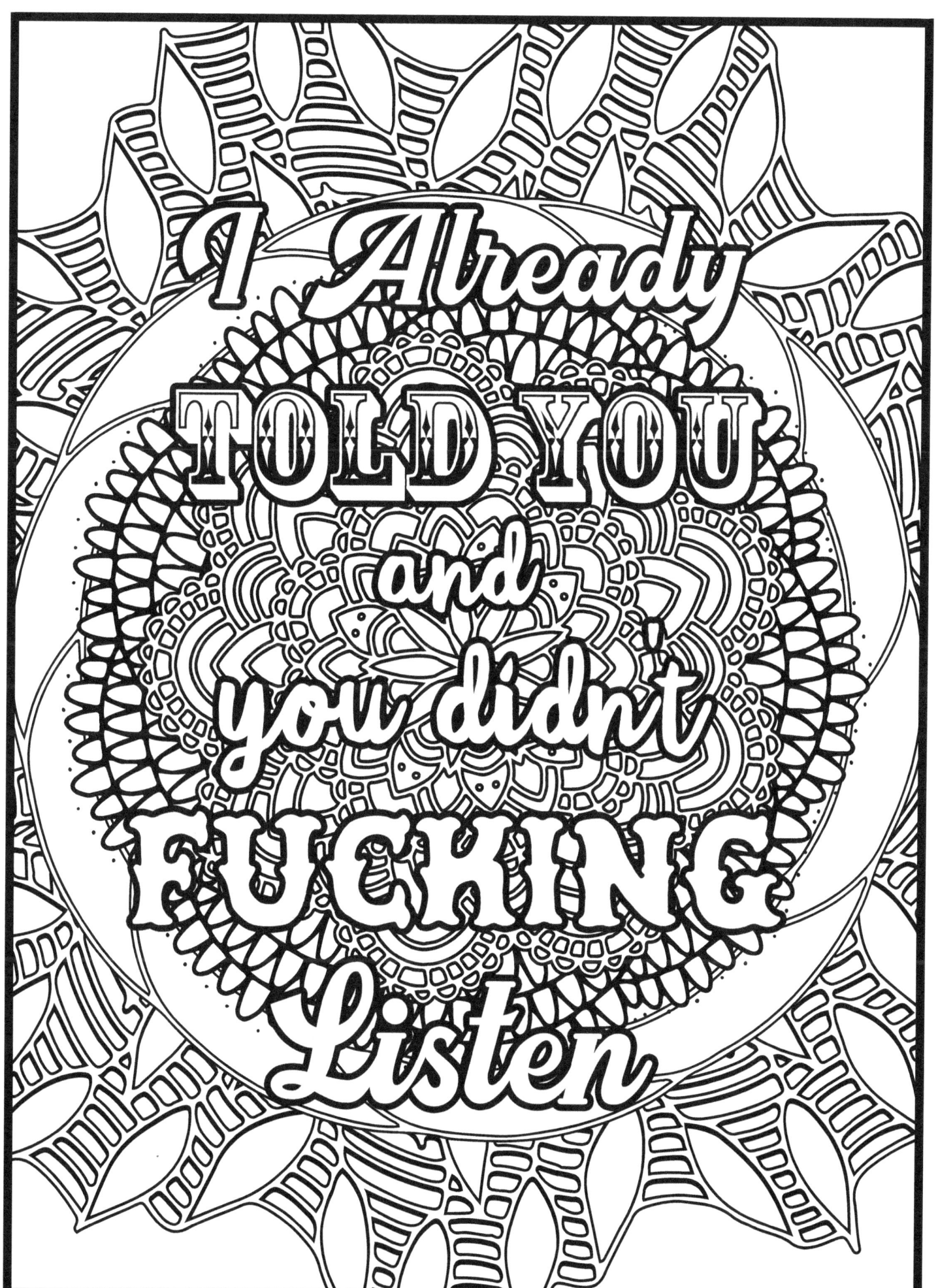

# Colorful

# Swearing Dreams

Swear Word Coloring Book for Adults

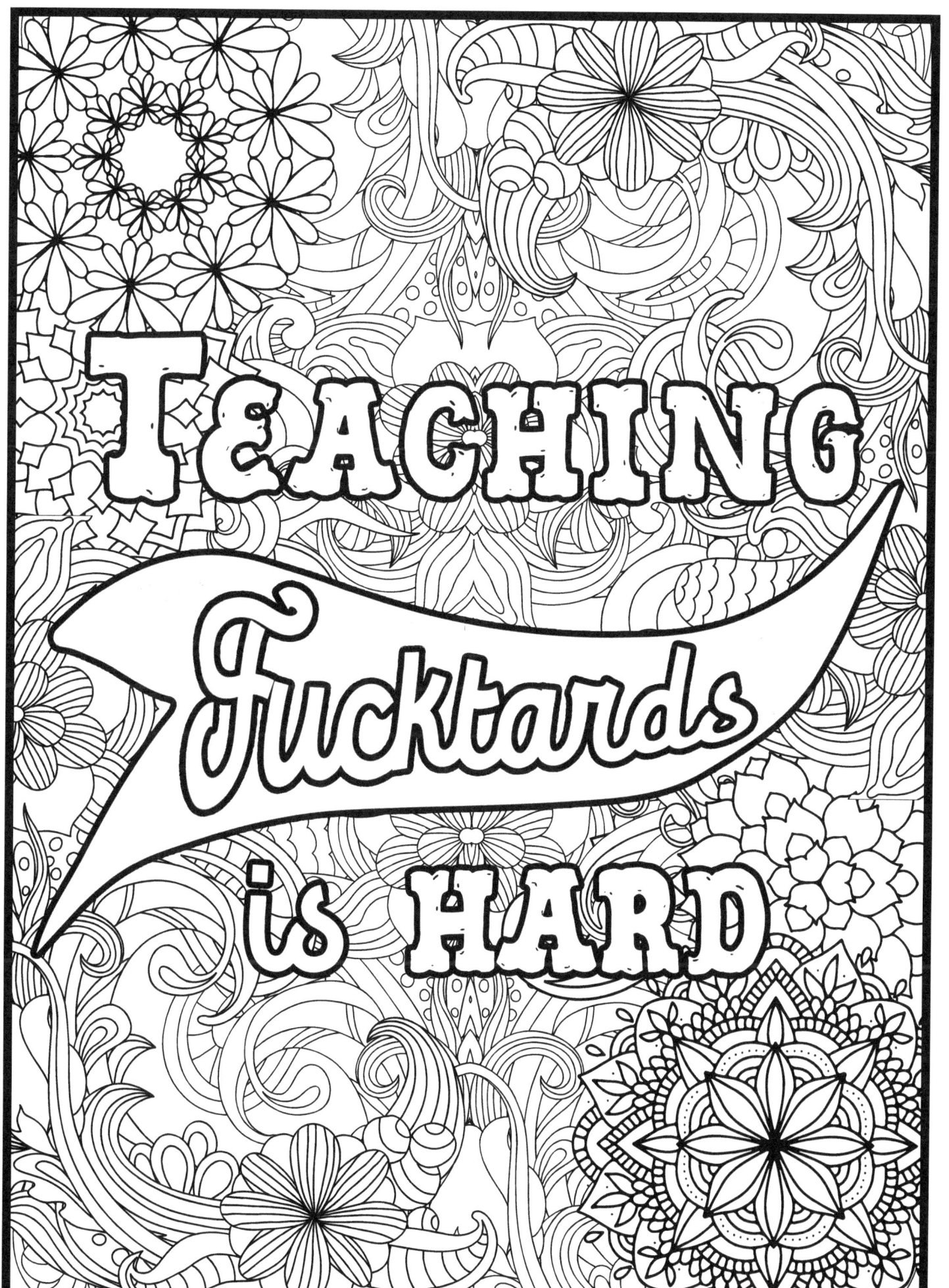

# Colorful Swearing Dreams

Swear Word Coloring Book for Adults

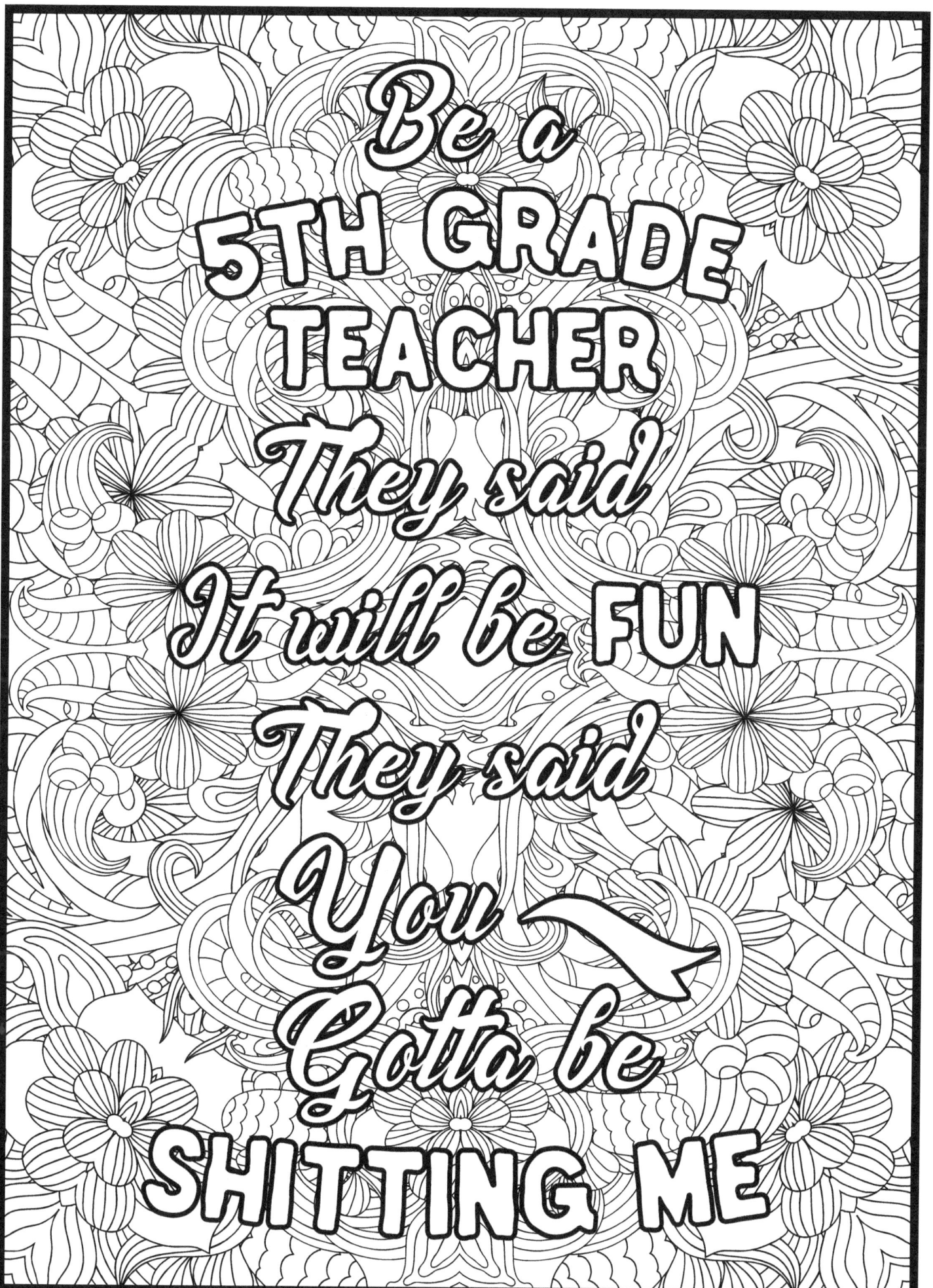

# Colorful Swearing Dreams

Swear Word Coloring Book for Adults

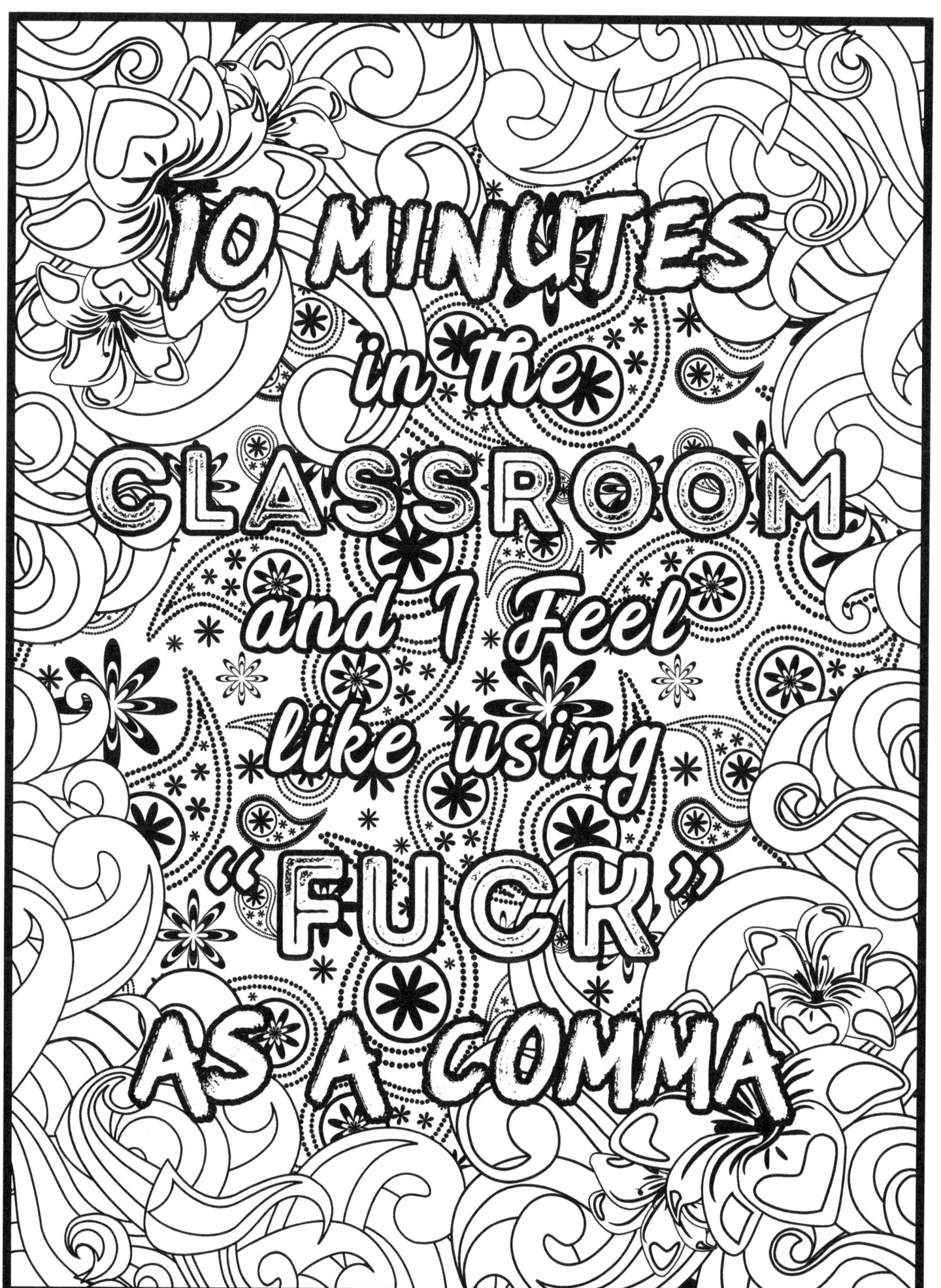

# Colorful Swearing Dreams

## Swear Word Coloring Book for Adults

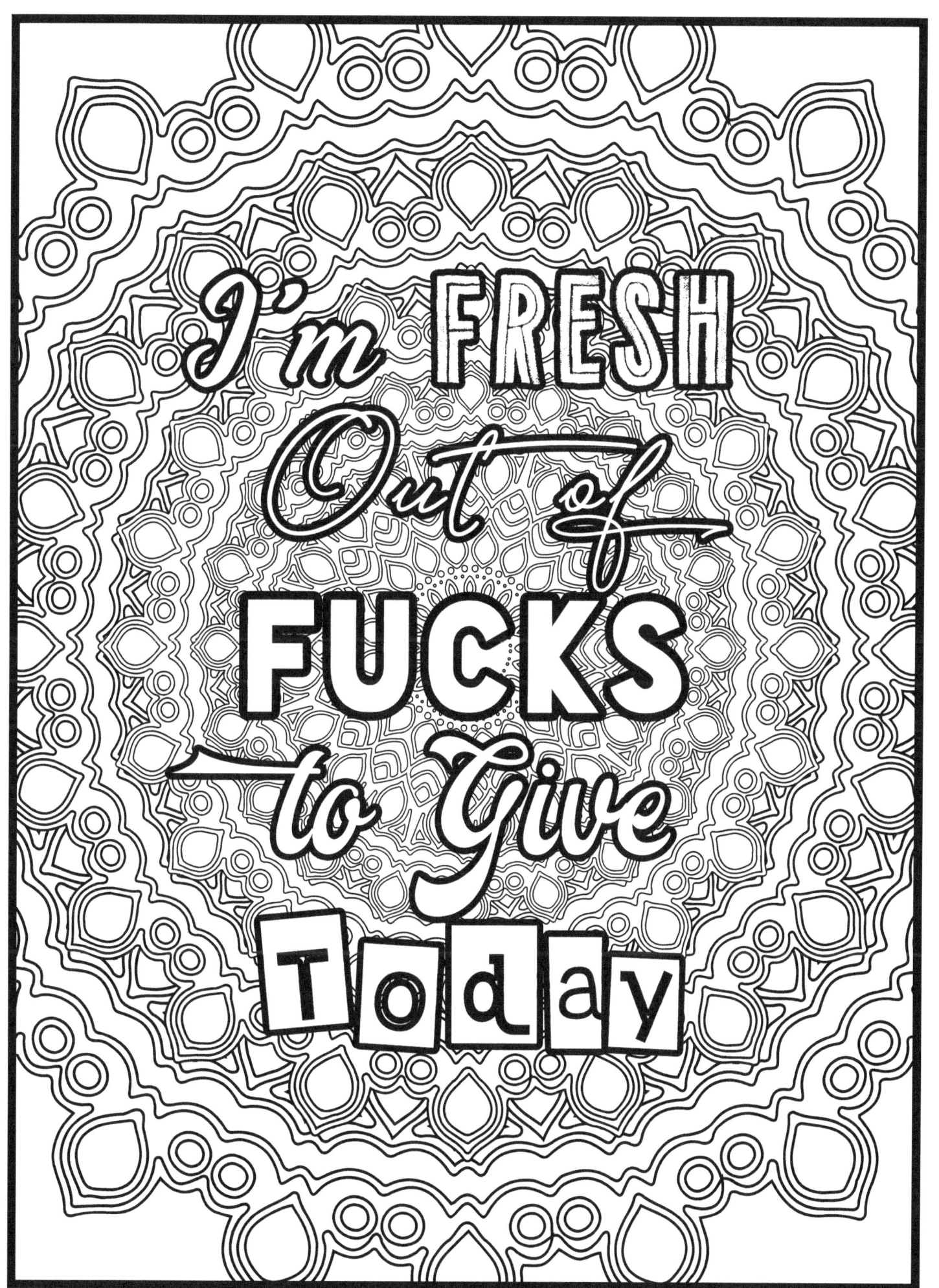

# Colorful Swearing Dreams

Swear Word Coloring Book for Adults

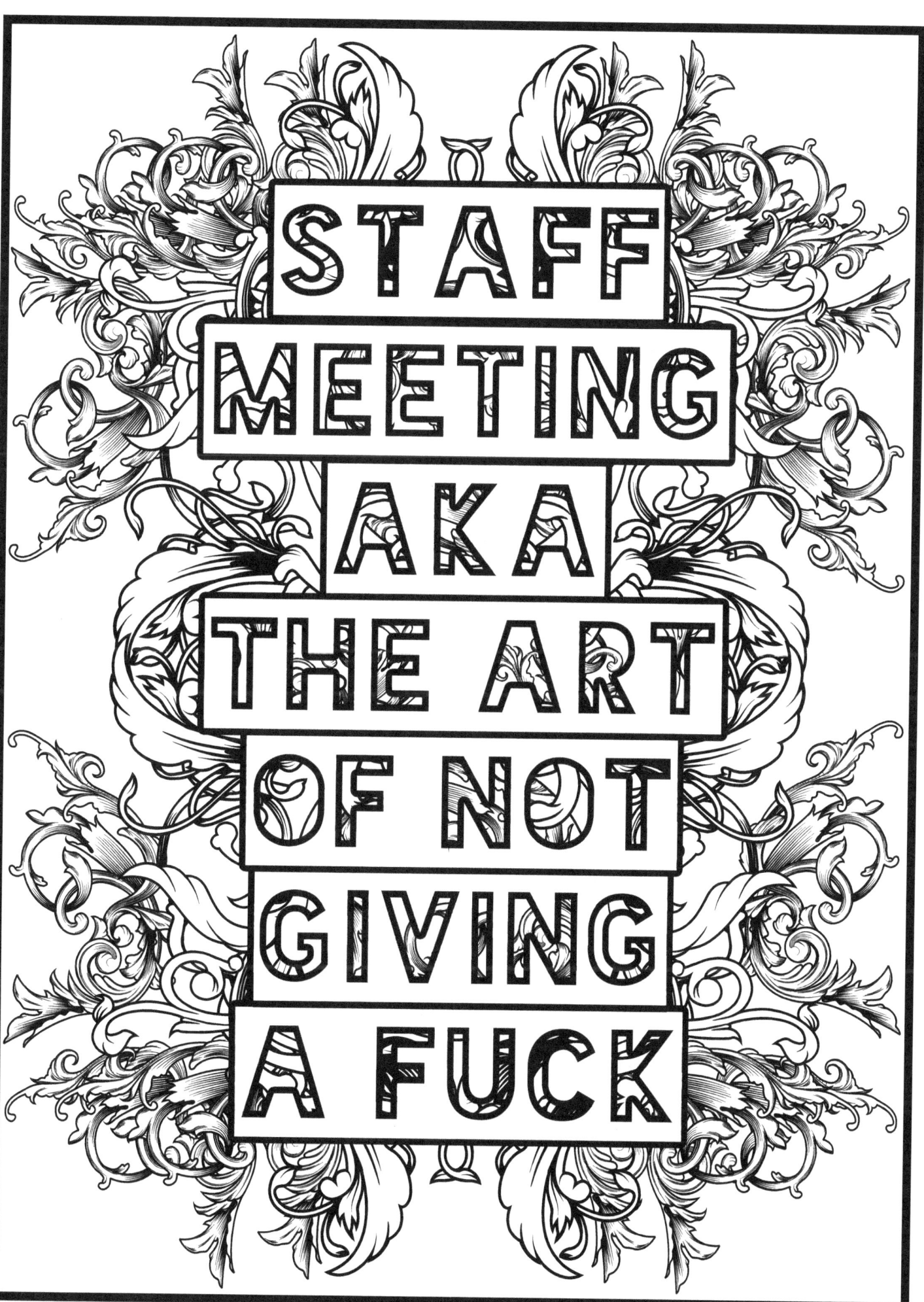

# Colorful Swearing Dreams

Swear Word Coloring Book for Adults

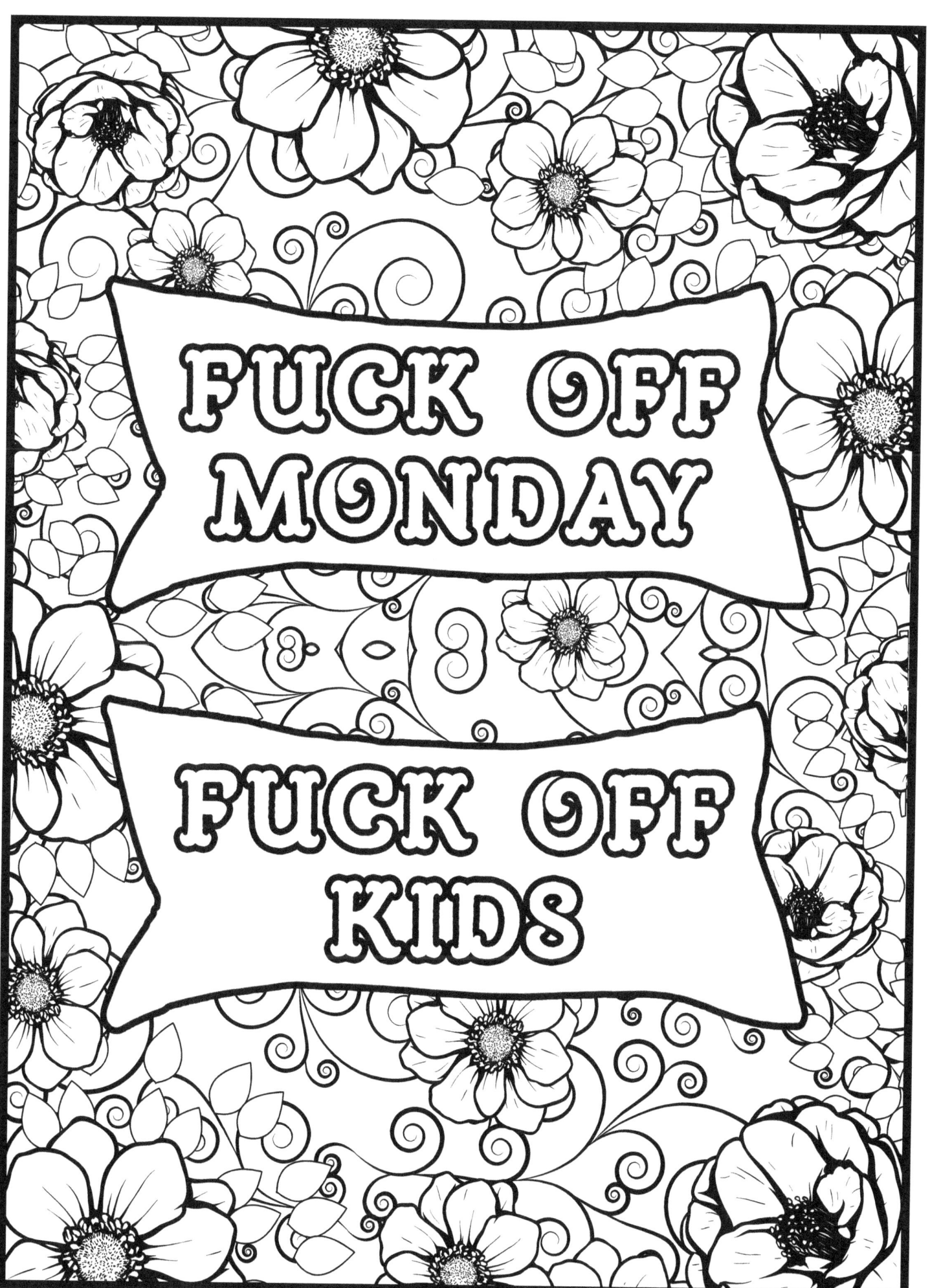

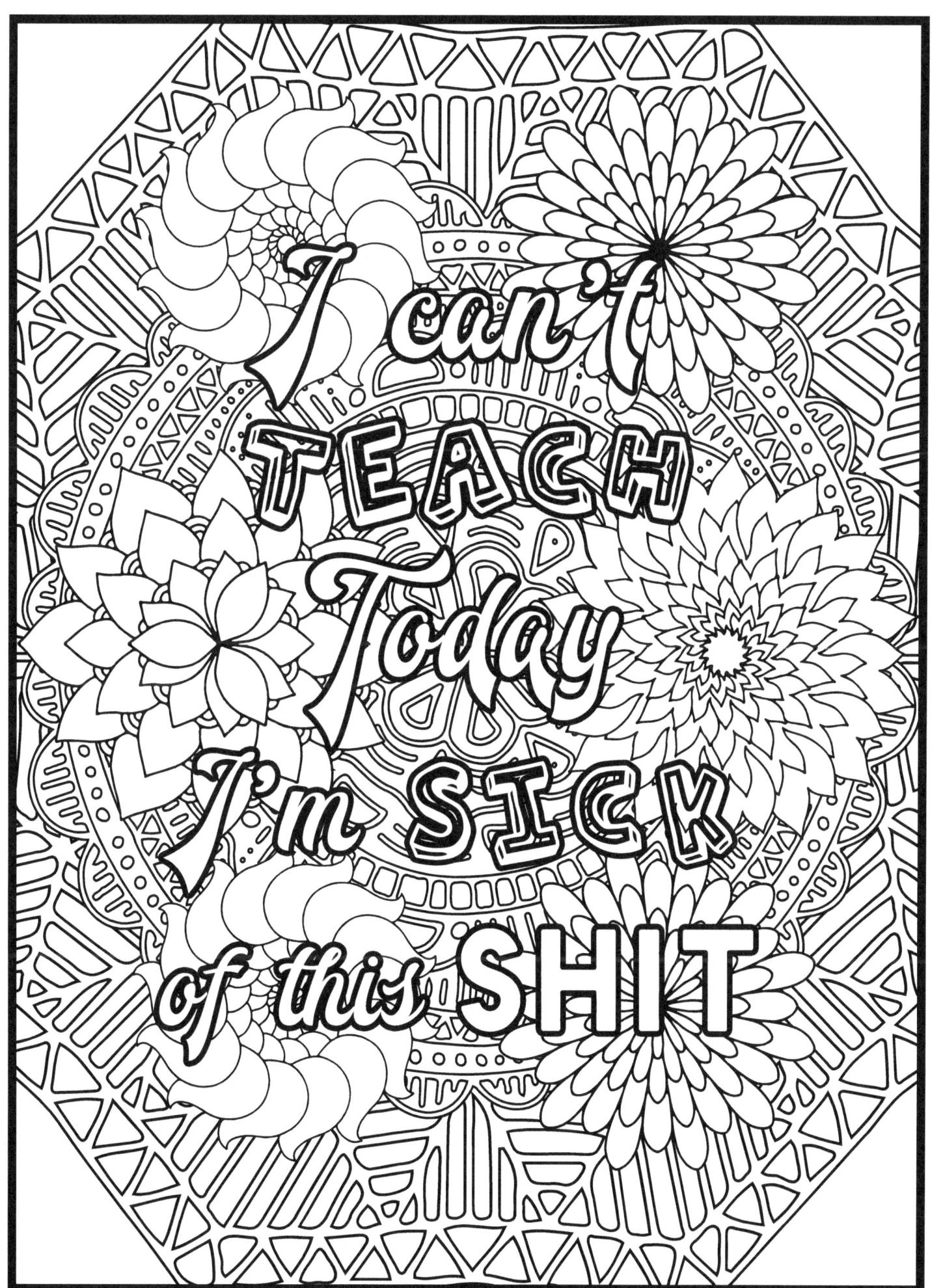

# Colorful Swearing Dreams

## Swear Word Coloring Book for Adults

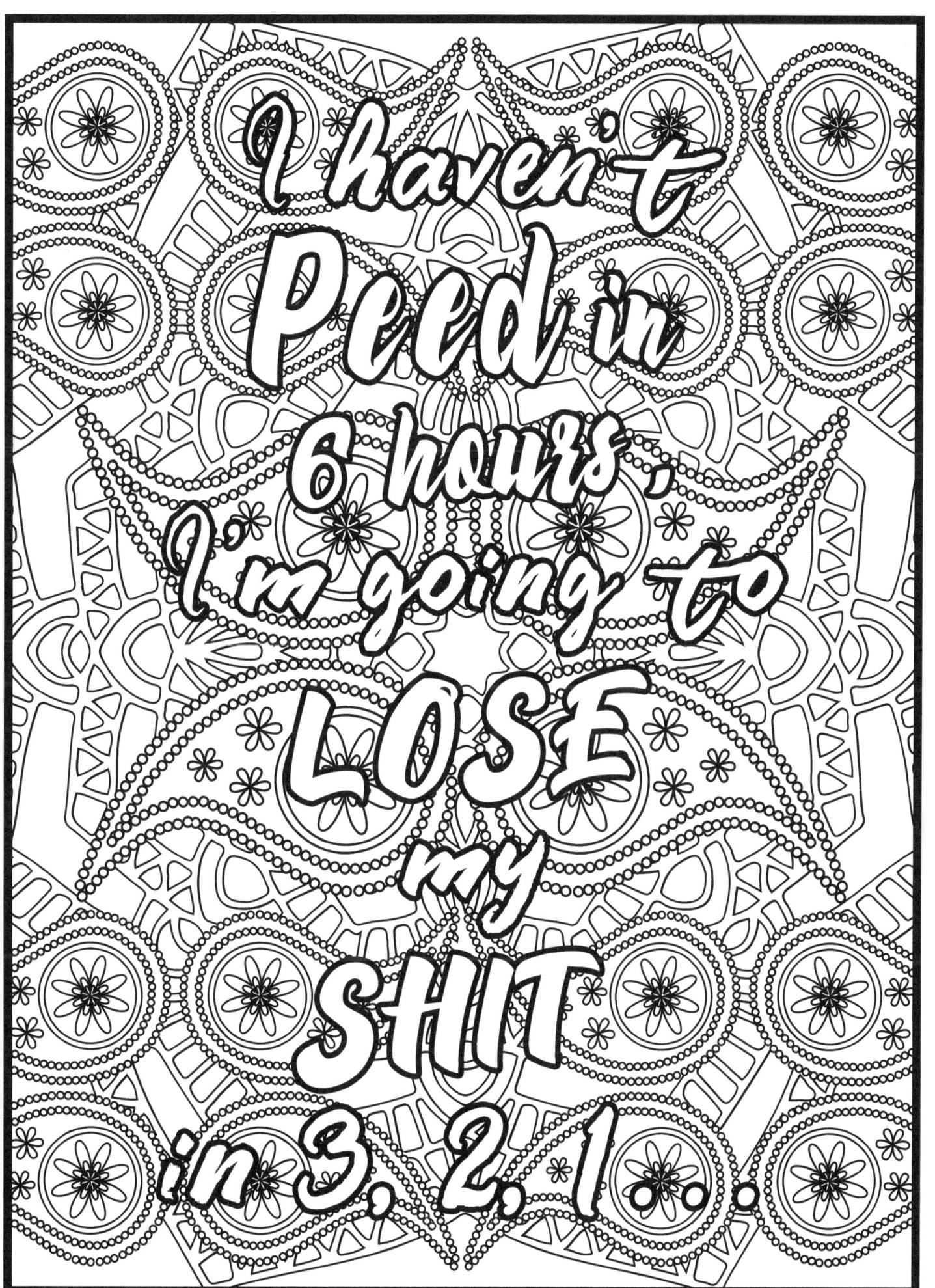

# Colorful Swearing Dreams

## Swear Word Coloring Book for Adults

# Colorful Swearing Dreams

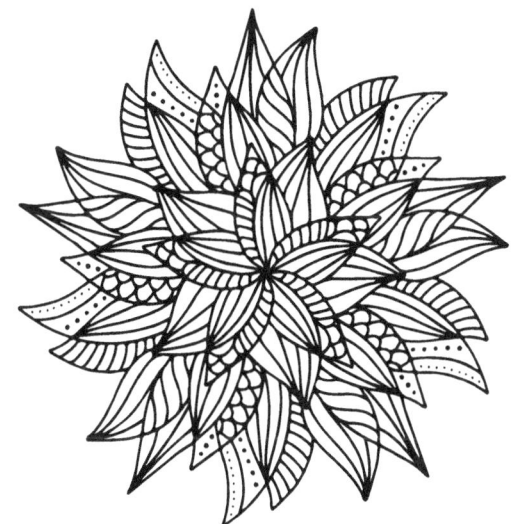

## How is your stress level now?

## Would you be kind enough to review our book?

Did the book allow you to put all the stress out of your mind, body and soul?
Hopefully you now feel fulfilled, relaxed and happy.

We sure put a lot of effort to provide you the best product possible that fits all your needs.

YOUR REVIEW is extremely valuable to us.
We don't see it as just a star rating, we read and study the feedbacks so we can
consistently improve our products to shape them how you want them to be.

We take pride in making quality products for your satisfaction.

That is why, we would really appreciate if you can take few minutes of your time and
leave us a review on our product's page.
That way, not only you will help other customers to make the right decision but
you will also allow us to make other quality products that can make funny & unique
gifts for your friends and family to just make them happy!

# Colorful Swearing Dreams

## Swear Word Coloring Book for Adults

www.ingramcontent.com/pod-product-compliance
Lightning Source LLC
Chambersburg PA
CBHW081021170526
45158CB00010B/3123